HOME IMPROVEMENTS

The Chapman Guide to
Negotiating Change With Your Spouse

GARY D. CHAPMAN, PH.D.

TYNDALE HOUSE PUBLISHERS, INC.

Carol Stream, Illinois

Visit Tyndale's exciting Web site at www.tyndale.com

TYNDALE and Tyndale's quill logo are registered trademarks of Tyndale House Publishers, Inc.

Home Improvements: The Chapman Guide to Negotiating Change with Your Spouse

Designed by Ron Kaufmann

Edited by Dave Lindstedt

Library of Congress Cataloging-in-Publication Data

Chapman, Gary D., date.
  Home improvements : the Chapman guide to negotiating change with your spouse / Gary D. Chapman.
     p. cm.
  Includes bibliographical references.
  ISBN-13: 978-1-4143-0015-3 (hc)
  ISBN-10: 1-4143-0015-8 (hc)
  1. Marriage—Religious aspects—Christianity. 2. Marital conflict—Religious aspects—Christianity. 3. Interpersonal—Religious aspects—Christianity. I. Title.
  BV835.C4577 2006
  646.7'8—dc22   2006021617

Printed in the United States of America

12   11   10   09   08   07   06
 7   6   5   4   3   2   1

TABLE OF CONTENTS

Introduction

After thirty years as a marriage counselor, I have drawn one firm conclusion: All married people wish their spouse would change. Sometimes, these desires go unexpressed but are refined and deepened in the process of daydreaming. The husband pictures his wife as having made the changes he desires, and he relishes this new creation. The wife dreams of a husband who will take out the garbage without being asked. These secretly nurtured visions of the perfect spouse become barriers to intimacy in the real world.

At the other extreme are husbands or wives who overtly declare their demands for change, usually in the heat of anger. Harsh language and brutal behavior reveal the intensity of their desire for change. One wife reported that her husband pushed her against the wall, and when she complained, he said, "When you start acting like a wife, I'll start treating you like one. Until then, you get what you deserve." Behind the words "start acting like a wife" were no doubt specific expectations he had that would require a change in her behavior. A wife who screams, "I am sick and tired of picking up after you; it's time you grew up," is revealing her expectations for change.

In between the two extremes of silent desire and brazen demands, thousands of couples live with unfulfilled expectations. If only their husband or wife would change, life would be so different. Sometimes they attempt to express their desires; other times, they simply give up in frustration.

What's the problem? Why is the desire for spousal change so universal, and yet the reality of change so rare? I believe the answer lies in three factors:

- We start at the wrong place.

- We fail to understand the power of love.

- We lack the skills to effectively communicate our desire for our spouse to change.

This book will answer the question, "How do I get my spouse to change—without manipulation?" In the next few pages, I will show you the right place to start, how to leverage the power of love, and how to develop the skills for requesting change.

This book is concise and to the point because I know you're busy. It is not a complicated book, but it is a powerful book. I believe that what you are about to read has the potential of bringing about the changes you desire in your spouse. It will not be easy to apply the principles I will teach you, but if you do, they will bear much fruit. In all my years of counseling, I have never known anyone who sincerely applied these principles who did not see significant change in the spouse's behavior.

The book is divided into three sections, each addressing one of the key issues mentioned above. I am going to talk to you as if you were sitting in my counseling office, and I am going to share with you what I have shared with hundreds of couples over the past three decades. If you're ready, so am I. Let's get started.

1

STARTING AT THE RIGHT PLACE

*I*nvariably, people who want their spouse to change start at the wrong place. A young man named Robert was one such person. He came alone to my office and told me that his wife, Sheila, would not come with him.

"What seems to be the nature of the problem?" I asked.

"For one thing, my wife is so disorganized. She spends half her life looking for her car keys. She never knows where to find anything because she can't remember where she put it. I'm not talking Alzheimer's—she's only thirty-five. I'm talking totally disorganized. I've tried to help her. I've made suggestions, but she's not open to anything I say. She says I'm controlling her. I'm not trying to control her. I just want to help make her life easier. If she would get more organized, it would certainly make my life easier, too. I waste a lot of time helping her find things she's lost."

I jotted some notes while Robert was talking, and when he was done, I asked, "Are there other problem areas?"

"Money. I have a good job. I make enough that we should be able to live comfortably, but not the way Sheila spends it. I mean, she makes no attempt to shop; she pays full price for everything. Like her clothes—if she would just buy them at the right season, they would be half price. We've gone for financial counseling, but she won't follow the financial planner's advice. Right now, we owe $5,000 on our credit card, and yet Sheila won't stop spending."

I nodded my head as I listened. "Are there other problem areas, Robert?"

"Well, yes. Sheila is just not interested in sex. I think she could live without it. If I didn't initiate it, we would never have sex. Even when I do, I'm often rejected. I thought sex was an important part of marriage, but apparently she doesn't feel that way."

As the session continued, Robert shared a few more of his frustrations about his wife's behavior. He said he had made every effort to get her to change, but he had seen few, if any, positive results. He was frustrated and at the point of hopelessness. He had come to me because he had read my books and thought that perhaps if I were to call his wife, she might talk to me and maybe I could get her to change. I knew from experience, however, that if Sheila came to my office, she would tell a different story than the one I'd heard from Robert. She would tell me about her problems with him. She would probably say that instead of being understanding, Robert is demanding and harsh with her. She would say, "If Robert would treat me with a little kindness and be a little romantic, I could be interested in sex." She would say, "I wish I could hear one compliment from him about some purchase I have made, rather than always condemning me for spending too much money." In essence, her perspective would be "If Robert would change, then I would change."

Is there hope for Robert and Sheila? Can they get the changes they desire in each other? I believe the answer is yes, but first they must radically change their approach. They are starting at the wrong place.

ANCIENT WISDOM

In my counseling practice, I have discovered that most of the relationship principles that really work are not new. Many are found in ancient literature, though they've often been overlooked for years. For example, the principle of starting at the right place can be found in a lesson that Jesus taught, commonly known as the Sermon on the Mount. I will paraphrase the quote to apply the principle directly to the marriage relationship: "Husband, why do you look at the speck of sawdust in your wife's eye and pay no attention to the plank in your own eye? Or, wife, how can you say to your husband, 'Let me take the speck out of your eye,' when all the time there is a plank in your own eye? You hypocrite, first take the plank out of your own eye, and then you will see clearly to remove the speck from your spouse's eye."[1]

The principle is clear: The place to start is getting the plank out of your own eye. Notice carefully that Jesus did not say, "There's nothing wrong with your mate. Leave him or her alone." In fact, he indicated that there is something wrong with your mate when he said, "Once you get the plank out of your own eye, then you can see more clearly to get the speck out of your spouse's eye."

Everyone needs to change. There are no perfect spouses—although I did hear once of a pastor who asked the question, "Does anyone know of a perfect husband?" One man in the back of the church raised his hand quickly and said, "My wife's first husband." My conclusion is that if there were any perfect husbands, they're all dead. I've never met a real live husband who didn't need to change. Nor have I met a perfect wife.

The most common reason people do not get the changes they desire in their spouse is that they start at the wrong place. They focus on their spouse's failures before they give attention to their own shortcomings. They see that little speck in their spouse's eye and begin to go after it by tossing out a suggestion. When that doesn't work, they overtly request a change. When that approach meets with resistance, they turn up the heat by demanding that their spouse change—or else. From there they move on to intimidation and manipulation. Even if they succeed in bringing about some change, it comes with deep resentment on the part of the spouse. This is not the kind of change that most people desire. Therefore, if you really want to see your spouse change, you must start by dealing with your own failures.

GETTING THE PLANK OUT OF YOUR OWN EYE

Dealing with our own failures first is not the way most of us have been trained to think. We're more likely to say, "If my spouse weren't like that, then I wouldn't be like this." "If my spouse didn't do that, then I wouldn't do this." "If my spouse would change, then I would change." Entire marriages have been built on this approach. One wife said, "If my husband would treat me with respect, then I would be able to be affectionate; but when he acts like I'm his slave, I want to run away and hope he'll never find me." To be honest, I empathize greatly with this wife; however, "waiting for my spouse to change" has led thousands of couples to an emotional state of hopelessness, which often ends in divorce when one or both spouses conclude, "He (or she) will never change; therefore, I'm getting out."

If we're honest with ourselves, we have to admit that waiting and hoping has not worked. We have seen little change unless it has been the result of manipulation—external pressure, either emotional or physical, that was designed to make a spouse uncomfortable enough to want to change. Unfortunately, manipulation creates resentment, and the marriage ends up worse after the change than it was before. If this has been your experience, as it was in the early years of my own marriage, then I hope you will be open to a different approach, one that works without creating resentment.

Learning to deal first with your own failures will not come easy. If I were to give you a sheet of paper, as I often do to those who come to me for counseling, and ask you to take fifteen minutes to make a list of the things you would like to see changed in your spouse, chances are you could make a rather formidable list. However, if I gave you another sheet of paper and asked you to take fifteen minutes to make a list of your own failures—things that you know need to be changed in the way you treat your spouse—my guess is that your list would be very short.

The typical husband's lists will have twenty-seven things wrong with his wife and only four things wrong with him. The wives' lists are not much different. One wife came back with a list of seventeen things that she wanted her husband to change, but the page of her own shortcomings was blank. She said, "I know you are not going to believe this, but I honestly can't think of a single thing I'm doing wrong."

I have to confess I was speechless. I had never met a perfect woman before. I thought about calling my secretary to bring in the camera: "Let's get a picture of this lady."

After about thirty seconds of silence, she said, "Well, I know what *he* would say."

"What's that?" I asked.

"He'd say that I am failing in the sexual area, but that's all I can think of."

I didn't say it, but the thought did run through my mind: *That's pretty major, even if it's the only thing you can think of.*

It's not easy to get the plank out of your own eye, but let me give you three steps that will help you do it:

STEP 1: ASK FOR OUTSIDE HELP

Most people will not be able to identify their own flaws without some outside help. We are so accustomed to our own ways of thinking and acting that we fail to recognize when they are dysfunctional and negative. Let me suggest some sources of help in identifying the plank in your own eye:

Talk to God

For some people, this might be uncomfortable, but I suggest you ask God's advice if you want some good insight. Your prayer might go something like this: "God, what *is* wrong with me? Where am I failing my spouse? What am I doing and saying that I shouldn't? What am I failing to do or say that I should? Please show me my failures." This simple prayer (or one like it) has been prayed and answered for thousands of years. Take a look at this prayer from the Hebrew Psalms, written in approximately 1000 BC by King David, Israel's second king: "Search me, O God, and know my heart; test me and know my anxious thoughts. Point out anything in me that offends you, and lead me along the path of everlasting life."[2] We can be certain that when we pray a prayer like this, God will answer.

If you're ready, take fifteen minutes to ask God to show you your failures in your marriage, then list whatever he brings to your mind. These may not be major moral failures, but could be words and actions that have not been loving and kind. Whatever things come to mind that have been detrimental to your marriage, write them down.

Here are the lists that one couple compiled after praying this prayer. (I suggest you complete your own list before looking at these.)

Husband

I watch too much TV.

I need to be more helpful with things around the house.

I don't use my time wisely.

I don't listen to her like I should.

I don't act kindly to her at times.

I don't talk things out with her.

I don't listen to her ideas.

Our time of sharing is sparse.

I have made her afraid to voice her views.

We don't pray together like we should.

Wife

I fail to encourage him.

I put myself and my needs above his needs.

I put him down at times.

I am not affectionate enough.

I expect him to do things the way I would.

I am sometimes rude and harsh in my speech.

I spend too much time on the computer.

I am not sensitive to my husband's love language.

I don't like to admit when I'm wrong.

I don't spend enough time with God.

I focus more time and energy on our son than on our marriage.

I hold on to wrongs from the past and use them in arguments.

I need to stop looking at his faults and look at mine.

Talk to Your Friends

In addition to talking with God, I suggest that you talk with a couple of friends who know you well and who have observed you and your marriage. Tell them that you are trying to improve your marriage and you want them to be completely honest with you. Tell them you are focusing on areas in which you need to improve in your own life. Ask them to give you honest feedback on whatever they have observed in your life, particularly the ways you respond to your spouse. Tell them that you will still be friends after they give you the truth—in fact, it's because of your friendship that you know you can trust them to be truthful with you. Don't argue with your friends. Simply write down whatever they tell you.

One friend said to a wife who had asked for input, "Do you really want me to be honest?" When the wife said yes, the friend said, "You are critical of your husband in front of other people. I have often felt sorry for your husband. I know it's embarrassing for him." The truth may be hard to hear (in some cases, it will be *very* hard), but if you don't hear it, you'll never take the necessary steps to change and you won't accomplish your goal of a better marriage.

A friend said to a husband who had asked for feedback, "My observation is that you often try to control your wife. I remember that just last week she was standing in the lobby of the church talking with another lady, and you walked up and said, 'We've got to go.' It was like you were her father telling her what she needed to do." Friends will often give you perceptions of yourself you have never imagined.

Talk to Your Parents and In-laws

If you are really courageous, and if your parents and your in-laws have had a chance to observe you and your marriage, you might ask them the same questions you asked your friends. Begin the conversation by telling them that you are trying to improve your marriage and you are focusing on the things that *you* need to change. Again, please don't argue with their comments. Simply write them down and express your appreciation for their honesty.

TALK TO YOUR SPOUSE

Now, if you really want to get serious, ask your spouse for the same information. You might say, "Honey, I really want to make our marriage better. I know that I have not been a perfect spouse, but I want to get better in the areas that are most important to you. So I want you to make a list of the things I've done, or failed to do, that have hurt you the most. Or perhaps it's things I've said or failed to say. I want to deal with my failures and try to make things different in the future." Don't argue with your spouse's list or rebuff the comments you are given. Simply receive them as information and thank your spouse for helping you become a better person.

STEP 2: REFLECT ON THE INFORMATION YOU HAVE GATHERED

When you have collected all the lists, what you will have in your hands is valuable information—about yourself and the way you relate to your spouse, from God's perspective and from the perspective of the people who are closest to you. Now it's time for you to come to grips with this information. This is not a time to develop rationalized defenses to the comments you've received. It is a time to accept the possibility that there is some truth in all these perspectives. From the lists you have received, make your own list of things that you agree are wrong in the way you treat your spouse.

I suggest that you personalize each sentence, starting with the word *I,* so that you are honestly reporting your own awareness of the flaws in your behavior. For example, "I recognize that I often lose my temper and say hurtful words to my spouse." Starting your sentences with *I* will help you keep it personal. Include statements about things that you should be doing but aren't, as well as things you are doing that you shouldn't. For example, in addition to the statement above about losing your temper and saying hurtful things to your spouse, you might also say, "I do not give my spouse enough positive, encouraging words."

In this time of reflection, be as honest as possible with yourself. You might even ask God to help you honestly evaluate your failures. Trying to justify yourself or excuse your behavior based on your spouse's behavior is a futile attempt at rationalization. Don't do it. You will never get the plank out of your own eye as long as you are excusing your failures.

STEP 3: CONFESSION

We have long known the emotional and spiritual power of confession. Confessing the things we've done wrong liberates us from the bondage of past failures and opens us up to the possibility for changed behavior in the future. I suggest that you begin by confessing your failures to God. Here is King David's confession, written after God showed David his failures. Your own confessions may not be expressed as poetically as David's, but you may find that his words of confession will help you express your own.

HAVE MERCY ON ME, O GOD, BECAUSE
    OF YOUR UNFAILING LOVE.

BECAUSE OF YOUR GREAT COMPASSION,
    BLOT OUT THE STAIN OF MY SINS.

WASH ME CLEAN FROM MY GUILT. PURIFY
    ME FROM MY SIN.

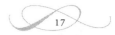

For I recognize my rebellion; it haunts me day and night.

Against you, and you alone, have I sinned; I have done what is evil in your sight.

You will be proved right in what you say, and your judgment against me is just.

For I was born a sinner—yes, from the moment my mother conceived me.

But you desire honesty from the womb, teaching me wisdom even there.

Purify me from my sins, and I will be clean; wash me, and I will be whiter than snow.

Oh, give me back my joy again; you have broken me—now let me rejoice.

Don't keep looking at my sins. Remove the stain of my guilt.

Create in me a clean heart, O God. Renew a loyal spirit within me.

Do not banish me from your presence,
    and don't take your Holy Spirit
    from me.

Restore to me the joy of your salvation,
    and make me willing to obey you.

Psalm 51:1-12, NLT

The word *confession* means, literally, "to agree with." When we confess to God, it means that we agree with him that what we have done or failed to do is wrong. Confession is the opposite of rationalization. Confession makes no attempt to minimize our wrongdoing but openly admits that our behavior is inexcusable.

The God who is revealed in the Bible is a God who stands ready to forgive those who admit their sins. Here is one brief quote: "If we confess our sins [to God], he is faithful and just and will forgive us our sins and purify us from all unrighteousness."[3]

The New Testament tells us that the reason God can forgive our wrongdoing and still be a God of justice is because Christ has paid the penalty for our failures. The ultimate penalty for wrongdoing is death. Because Christ took that penalty in our place, God is willing to forgive us. The penalty has already been paid by Christ. That is the central message of the Christian faith.

However, confession of wrongdoing needs to be broader than simply admitting your failures to God. You also must confess to the person you have wronged. In marriage, that is your spouse. Having confessed to God, you should now have the courage to confess to your spouse. Your confession might go something like this: "I've been thinking about us, and I realize that in a lot of ways I have failed you. I sat down the other day and made a list of the things I feel I have done that are wrong. I have asked God to forgive me for each of these things, and if you have a few minutes, I'd like to share my list with you and ask if you would forgive me, as well. I really want the future to be different, and I think this is where I need to start."

Most spouses will be willing to forgive when they hear an honest confession. If there has been a drastic violation of your marriage vows, it may take time for trust to be rebuilt. But the rebuilding process starts with an act of genuine confession.[4]

If you have gone to your parents or in-laws to ask for their input about your failures in your marriage, you might also want to confess your failures to them and ask for their forgiveness. Such confessions will go a long way toward rebuilding trust, respect, and a positive relationship with them. Even if you did not ask for their input but you know they are aware of your marital failures, I would encourage you to confess to your parents and in-laws.

COMMON QUESTIONS ABOUT STARTING AT THE RIGHT PLACE

Having read these ideas about starting at the right place, you may have questions floating in your mind. When I present this concept at my marriage seminars, I hear some common questions. For example, a wife in the Midwest said, "I understand what you are saying. I know that I need to get the plank out of my own eye, but I don't think you fully understand my situation. What if your spouse really *is* the problem?"

I thought for a moment and responded, "Let's assume that your husband is 95 percent of the problem. That would leave only 5 percent for you. But even if the problem is mostly with your spouse, you wouldn't say that you are perfect, would you?"

"Oh no," she said. "No one is perfect."

"Well, if we're not perfect, then we're imperfect, right?"

"Right . . ."

"So let's assume your husband is 95 percent imperfect and you are only 5 percent imperfect. What I'm suggesting is that if *you* want to improve your marriage, and if *you* want to see changes in your husband, the place for you to start is with *your* 5 percent. Your marriage will immediately be 5 percent better, and you will be freed from the guilt of past failures and emotionally liberated to be a positive influence on your husband."

I'm not sure she was totally satisfied with my answer, but she did nod her head and say, "Okay, that makes a lot of sense."

Rob, a middle-aged husband from Birmingham, asked me another question: "If I confess my failures to God and to my wife, do you think she will come back in a few days and confess her failures to me?"

I wish I could have answered affirmatively and with confidence, but in all honesty, I had to say, "I don't know. But that would be nice, wouldn't it?"

Rob nodded as tears coursed down his cheeks.

"I'm not even certain that your wife will forgive you," I continued. "I wish I could guarantee that, but the fact is we can't predict human behavior. She may be so deeply hurt and angered that she cannot honestly forgive you at the moment. You must be patient with her and give her time to process your confession."

What I did guarantee Rob, and can guarantee you, is that when you confess your failures in your marriage, you have removed the first barrier to marital growth. Confession creates a climate that fosters positive change. You cannot erase your past failures, but you can agree that what you did, or failed to do, was wrong, and you can sincerely ask for forgiveness. In so doing, you are starting at the right place.

"But if she doesn't forgive me," Rob said, "how can there be hope for change?"

I reminded him that confession of one's failures is only the first step in seeking change. Your spouse's immediate response may not be the ultimate response. A woman who initially said to her husband, "I don't know that I can ever forgive you; too much has happened, and the hurt is too deep," three months later said, "I didn't know that I would ever be able to forgive you, but today I want you to know that the past is the past. I no longer hold it against you." What happens after the confession will have an impact on whether or not your spouse chooses to forgive you, but we'll discuss what comes next when we get to chapter 2.

The process described in this first chapter will obviously take some time. I doubt that the confession phase can be completed in less than a month. However, I want you to read the rest of the book now because I want you to see where we're going.

I can assure you that, in the end, I am going to give you the key to getting your spouse to change without manipulation.

After your confessions have been made, you have taken the first step in creating an atmosphere for requesting change from your spouse. I was honest with you from the beginning when I said that the road to change is not easy. I am fully aware that confessing your failures to God and to your spouse is a major accomplishment. However, few things are more important than confession for maintaining both mental and marital health. When you confess your failures, it is like emptying your conscience and cleansing it of all the guilt that goes along with those failures. Living with a clean conscience will keep you mentally and relationally alert, and it will free you from the bondage of past failures. After you have confessed, you will feel better about yourself, and your spouse will begin to look at you with more respect and dignity because you have been strong enough to deal with your own failures.

After confession, you will likely feel emotionally elated because a burden has been lifted and because you are being authentic with your spouse. There is something exhilarating about being honest and dealing with our failures. However, please don't jump to the conclusion that you can now request change and expect your spouse to comply. There is another major ingredient that must be added before you are ready to take that step. It has to do with the power of emotional love. Read on.

~

TAKING ACTION

1. In the past, what has been your approach to your own failures in your marriage?

    ___ blame them on my spouse

    ___ deny them

    ___ admit them, but refuse to change

    ___ say, "I'll change when you change."

    ___ fully confess my failures and ask for forgiveness

    ___ other

2. If you are willing, say to God, "I know I'm not perfect, so where have I failed in my marriage?" Make a list of what comes to your mind.

3. If you are willing to seek outside help, write the date you asked for input from the following people:

    _____ God

    _____ close friends

    _____ parents

    _____ in laws

    _____ spouse

4. Admitting your failures and asking forgiveness may be difficult, especially if you believe that your spouse is 95 percent of the problem. But would you be willing to *start at the right place* and see what happens? If so, write the dates when you made your list _____ and verbally confessed your failures to your spouse _____.

2

*Y*our desire to see change in your spouse is most likely correlated with a desire to meet some need in your own life. Regardless of culture, human beings are by nature egocentric. We think the world revolves around us. Meeting our own needs is the motivation behind much of our behavior. Robert wanted Sheila to become more organized so that she would not spend so much of her time looking for things, but he also admitted that part of his motivation was that he did not want to waste his own time helping her. He wanted her to be more interested in sex because his needs were not being met. He wanted her to spend less money so that he would feel that he was a good provider and they could live within their means. On the other hand, Sheila desired to hear from Robert words of affirmation in order to enhance her own self-esteem. His condemning words cut deeply at her self-respect.

A concern for one's own well-being is natural and healthy. In fact, if we did not feed ourselves and get proper sleep and exercise, we would not be able to live. We are responsible for seeking to meet our own physical and emotional needs. At the same time, we are also designed for relationships. Those who live in isolation will never reach their full potential in society. Relationships call us to get outside of ourselves. If meeting our own needs becomes the central theme of our lives, we will never have good relationships.

Successful relationships require that we become interested in the well-being of another person. It is taking our natural desire to meet our own needs, turning it outward toward someone else, and using the same amount of energy to meet his or her needs. The word to describe this other-centered attitude is *love*. In this sense, the song is true: *Love makes the world go round.*[1] Without love, society would not continue. In a marriage relationship, I know of nothing more important than love. Where there is love, change is inevitable. Without love, positive change seldom occurs.

Reflect on the stage of life when you and your spouse were "in love." Is it not true that you were willing to do anything for your lover's benefit—climb the highest mountain, swim the deepest ocean, stop smoking, learn to dance? Whatever desire he or she expressed, you were willing to attempt. Why were you so open to change? I believe it was because your emotional need for love was being met so fully. It is true that *love stimulates love.*

In time, however, the emotional obsession you had for each other faded, and your egocentric natures took over. Both you and your spouse began focusing on getting your own needs met. Ironically, the result was that neither of you was satisfied. The nature of egocentric living is disappointment and hurt, which leads to anger, resentment, and bitterness. Such is the plight of thousands of married couples. In order for this to change, there must be a return to love—not the euphoric state of being "in love," but the conscious choice to look out for the best interests of the other person. Love requires a fundamental change of perspective. It goes against our natural bent toward selfishness, but it is the most powerful weapon in the world for good. It radically changes the climate of a marriage.

The attitude of love must find behavioral structures through which to be expressed. In my own marriage, these structures were formed by asking my wife the following questions:

"How may I help you?"

"What can I do that would make your life easier?"

"How can I be a better husband to you?"

When I was willing to ask those questions and let Karolyn's answers guide me in how I expressed my love to her, our marriage was reborn.

Through thirty years of marriage counseling, I have helped hundreds of couples discover how to connect with each other emotionally by choosing to walk the road of love. In 1992, I wrote a book called *The Five Love Languages,* which has helped literally hundreds of thousands of couples to reconnect and create a positive emotional climate in their marriages.[2] Of the five love languages, everyone has a primary love language. One of these styles of communication speaks more deeply to each of us emotionally than the other four. We like all of them to varying degrees, but there's usually one we prefer above the others, one that we wouldn't give up for anything. That is what makes us feel genuinely loved. When our spouse "speaks" to us in our primary love language, our love tanks fill up and we feel secure. The key is to discover your spouse's primary love language and give him or her heavy doses of it while sprinkling in the other four love languages as cherries on top of the sundae. I have never seen a marriage that was not improved when one spouse or both chose to follow this path.

To help you get started, I will briefly summarize the five love languages and illustrate why it is so important to learn your spouse's primary love language:

LOVE LANGUAGE #1:
WORDS OF AFFIRMATION

For some people, words of affirmation are what make them *feel* loved. Choosing to focus on the positive and to verbalize affirmation for those things you appreciate about your spouse will tend to motivate him or her to noble behavior. If your spouse's primary love language is words of affirmation, look for even the slightest opportunity to offer some simple, affirming words:

"You look nice in that dress."

"Oh, do you ever look sharp tonight."

"I really appreciate the meal."

"Thanks for taking out the garbage."

"I want you to know I do not take you for granted."

"I really appreciate the fact that you cleaned the kitchen tonight."

"Thanks for mowing the grass; the yard really looks nice."

"I appreciate your putting gas in my car. And thanks for getting the bugs off the windshield."

Affirming words may also focus on your spouse's personality traits:

"I noticed how you spent time with Rebecca last night. She seemed to be upset. I really appreciate the fact that you take time for people."

"I don't think I've told you this lately, but I really appreciate the fact that when I come home, you are always so encouraging and excited about my being here. That means a lot to me."

"I appreciate the spontaneity of your personality. You make my life interesting."

"The methodical way in which you attack problems is such a gift. I appreciate the way you make my life easier by solving so many of my problems."

Words of affirmation may also focus on the person's physical characteristics:

"Your hair looks nice."

"I love the twinkle in your eye."

"Have I told you lately that your breasts are beautiful?"

"Look at those muscles. Wow!"

"The blue of your eyes reminds me of a calm lake in the mountains."

Affirming words give life; condemning words bring death. Many couples have destroyed their marriage by using condemning, judgmental, harsh, cutting words. That can be changed when one spouse chooses to stop the flow of negativity and begin the flow of loving words.

LOVE LANGUAGE #2: GIFTS

My academic background is in anthropology, the study of cultures. No one has yet found a culture in which gift giving is not an expression of love. A gift says, "He was thinking about me. Look what he got for me." Gifts are a physical, visible token of thoughtfulness and care.

A gift need not be expensive. After all, it's the thought that counts, right? Actually, it is more than the thought left in your mind that counts; it is the thoughtful gift that results from the thought in your mind that makes the difference. Most of us could learn a great deal from observing our children. Children are masters of gift giving, and most of the time it costs them nothing. They make imaginary strawberry pies and ask you to join them in eating. They make cars out of paper towel tubes and buttons and give them to you as a gift. They run to you with a flower, present it with a smile, and say, "I got this for you." Where along the way to adulthood did we lose this spirit of gift giving?

I believe that anyone can learn to give gifts. It requires an awareness that gift giving is one of the fundamental languages of love, and you must decide to speak that language to your spouse. It's not what the gift costs but your thoughtfulness that matters. Make your wife a love card out of the various colored papers that come across your desk. Write words of affirmation on the card and give it to her on Valentine's Day—or better yet, on an "unspecial" day. Of course, not all gifts should be free. Listen to your spouse's comments about things he or she might like. If your spouse expresses a desire for something, make a note of it. Three weeks later, surprise your mate by presenting it to him or her after dinner.

LOVE LANGUAGE #3: ACTS OF SERVICE

"Actions speak louder than words." For some people, that is certainly true. Doing something that you know your spouse will like is a deep expression of love. Cooking meals, washing dishes, vacuuming the floors, mowing the lawn, washing the cars, doing laundry, cleaning the bathroom, changing the baby's diaper—all these are acts of service. Yes, they require time, effort, energy, and sometimes skill, but if your spouse's primary love language is acts of service, you will strongly communicate your love whenever you do something that you know your spouse will like.

In household responsibilities, we tend to be creatures of habit. We fall into patterns of behavior—he cooks, she washes dishes; she does the laundry, he mows the grass; he keeps the cars filled with gas, she makes sure the clothes are clean. We find our niche and stick with it. Of course, there is a positive aspect to all this. Typically, we will do the things that we feel best equipped to do, and if we do them with a positive spirit for the benefit of each other, we are speaking the language of love.

If the chores and responsibilities are already well established at your house, you can enhance your expression of love to your spouse by doing something that is not normally on your list. Be advised that your spouse might not understand or fully appreciate your efforts, as depicted in the following dialogue:

"Honey, would you like me to clean the bathrooms tonight?"

"Are you saying that I'm not keeping the bathrooms clean?"

"No, I think you're doing a great job. I just thought it might be nice if I did something to help you."

Be prepared that your spouse might not be overly enthusiastic at first. Perhaps he or she is still wondering if you are telling the truth. But once you have completed the task, you are likely to hear some words of affirmation.

LOVE LANGUAGE #4: QUALITY TIME

Quality time is much more than being in the same room or the same house with your spouse. It involves giving your spouse your undivided attention. It is sitting on the couch with the TV off, looking at each other and talking. It's taking a walk down the road, just the two of you. It is going out to eat and looking at each other and talking. Have you ever noticed how in a restaurant you can almost always tell the difference between dating couples and married couples? Dating couples will look at each other and talk; married couples sit quietly and eat. For the dating couple, it is quality time; for the married couple, it is meeting a basic physical need.

Why not turn your meal times into expressions of love by giving each other your undivided attention, talking and listening?

Begin by sharing the events of the day, but don't stop there. Talk about things that might be troubling your spouse, or desires that he or she has for the future. Once our spouses sense that we are interested in what they are thinking and feeling, they will not only talk more freely but also feel loved.

If you would like to shock your spouse with an expression of quality time, the next time your spouse walks into the room while you are watching TV, hit the mute button and turn and look at your spouse, giving him or her your undivided attention. If your spouse starts talking, flip the TV off and engage in conversation. If he or she walks out of the room without talking, you may go back to your TV program, but the simple act of making yourself available for quality time communicates that your spouse is more important to you than anything on television. Quality time is a powerful language of love.

LOVE LANGUAGE #5: PHYSICAL TOUCH

We have long known the emotional power of physical touch. All research indicates that babies who are affectionately touched fare better emotionally than babies who are not touched. The same is true of adults. If you have ever walked the halls of a home for the elderly, you have seen the outstretched hands of people who are longing to be touched. A handshake, a hug, a pat on the back would fill the love tank of many a lonely person.

In marriage, physical touch is one of the fundamental languages of love. Holding hands while you give thanks for a meal, putting your hand on your spouse's shoulder as you sit watching television, embracing each other when you meet after being apart, sexual intercourse, kissing—sometimes a peck, sometimes with passion—any touch, as long as it is affectionate, is a deep expression of love.

I remember a woman who said to me, "Of all the things my husband does, nothing is more important than the kiss on the cheek he gives me when he comes home from work. It doesn't matter how bad his day has been or how bad my day has been.

When he comes to greet me with a kiss before going to the television or the refrigerator, everything seems better." A man at one of my seminars said, "I never leave the house without getting a hug from my wife, which she initiates. And when I return, the first thing she does is give me a hug. Some days, her hugs are the only positive thing that happens, but they are enough to keep me going."

DISCOVERING YOUR PRIMARY LOVE LANGUAGE

In order to discover your primary love language, ask yourself what you complain about most often to your spouse. Your complaints reveal your love language. If every so often you say to your spouse, "We never spend any time together. We are like two ships passing in the night," you are communicating that your love language is quality time. If your spouse returns from a trip and you say, "You mean you didn't bring me anything?" you are revealing that your love language is gifts. If you hear yourself saying to your spouse, "You don't ever touch me. If I didn't touch you, I don't think we would ever touch," you are revealing that your love language is physical touch. If you often say to your spouse, "I don't ever do anything right," you are revealing that your love language is words of affirmation. If you hear yourself saying, "You don't ever help me around here. I mean, I have to do everything. If you loved me, you would do something around here," your primary love language is acts of service. If you have no complaints, it means that your spouse is speaking your primary love language, even though you may not know what it is.

How do you discover your spouse's primary love language? Listen to his or her complaints. Typically we get defensive when our spouse complains. If a husband says, "I don't understand why you can't keep this house halfway decent. It looks like a pigpen," his wife is likely to explode in angry words or burst into tears. However, her husband is giving her valuable information about his primary love language—acts of service. Listen to your spouse's complaints and you will learn what makes him or her feel loved.

The key to creating a positive emotional climate in a marriage is learning to speak each other's primary love language and speaking it regularly. My wife's love language is acts of service. That's why I vacuum floors, wash dishes, clean blinds, and fold clothes. I am not by nature a doer; I would much rather talk or listen. But I know that, for my wife, actions speak louder than words.

The other day, my wife said in passing, "The blinds are looking pretty dusty." I got the message, and I made a mental note. Two mornings later at about six o'clock, before I left to lead a marriage seminar, I was in the dining room vacuuming the blinds when Karolyn walked in and asked, "What are you doing?"

I said, "Honey, I'm making love."

She responded, "You have got to be the greatest husband in the world."

My primary love language is words of affirmation. Karolyn filled my love tank while I filled hers. It took thirty minutes and a little effort to vacuum blinds at six o'clock on Friday morning, but it was a small price to pay to live with a happy woman. Her response to me took less than six seconds, but for me those words of affirmation meant more than a thousand gifts.

From time to time, someone complains to me: "But what if my spouse's love language is something that just doesn't come naturally for me?" I always respond, "So?" Learning to speak a second language may not be easy, but the effort is well worth it. To be honest, vacuuming floors, washing dishes, and dusting blinds do not come naturally for me, but I have learned to speak my wife's love language because meeting her emotional need for love is important to me.

So where do you begin? I suggest you start where you are. If you grew up in a family that was not touchy-feely and you are married to someone whose love language is physical touch, start by touching yourself. Put one hand on top of the other, or rest your hand on your elbow or shoulder. Touch your knee or pat yourself on the thigh. When you become comfortable touching yourself, imagine putting your arm on your spouse's back for three seconds, or giving your spouse a small pat on the back. Practice these motions alone. Picture yourself touching your spouse casually and naturally. Then, one day, with all the courage you can muster, walk up to your spouse, pat him or her on the back, and see what kind of response you get. Your spouse may be surprised, but you will be on your way to mastering your spouse's love language. Next time—and the time after that—will be even easier.

If your spouse's love language is words of affirmation and you are not a verbal person, get a notebook and begin to write phrases and sentences that express positive affirmation to your spouse. If you can't think of anything, listen to what other people say and emulate that. Read magazines and books and record the expressions of love that you find. Next, stand in front of the mirror and read these things aloud to yourself. Become comfortable hearing these words come out of your mouth. When you're ready, pick one of these statements, walk up behind your spouse, and speak your chosen words of affirmation. You will have "broken the sound barrier" and made it progressively easier to speak words of affirmation. By the fourth or fifth time, you will start to become comfortable looking your spouse in the eye when you speak these words of affirmation.

If you decide to make the effort, you can learn to speak your spouse's primary love language. When you do, it will meet his or her most basic emotional need in the most effective way possible. Once you start speaking your spouse's primary love language, you can sprinkle in the other four languages as well for extra emotional credit.

You may be thinking, *So, what does all this talk about love have to do with getting my spouse to change?* I'm glad you asked, because unless you understand the answer to that question, you are not likely to see significant changes in your spouse. All of us have basic emotional needs, including the need for security, significance, freedom, self-worth, and love. When these emotional needs are not met, we become emotionally frustrated. This frustration may express itself in depression, anxiety, resentment, or withdrawal. In a state of emotional frustration, we are almost never open to our spouse's suggestions or requests. Typically, we interpret such requests as criticism. We may explode, retaliate, or withdraw, but we are not likely to change.

The most fundamental of all emotional needs is the need to feel loved. When we feel unloved, the whole world looks dark. Conversely, when our love tank is full and we genuinely feel loved by our husband or wife, the whole world looks bright. Life becomes an adventure, and we don't want to miss out on the excitement. In this positive state of mind, we are open to change, and the person to whom we are most responsive is the person who is filling our love tank.

When your spouse's love tank is full, he or she will be much more open to the changes that you desire, especially if you are the one who is filling your spouse's love tank. You have created a climate where change is not only possible but also likely.

Will it be easy to learn to speak your spouse's primary love language? Probably not, but the results are worth the effort.

When I met Brian and Joanne, they had been married for thirty-three years—but not thirty-three happy years. In fact, in Brian's words, "The last twenty years have been utterly miserable. We have lived in the same house and tried to be humane, but we really haven't had a marriage for the last twenty years."

With that revelation, I was looking at Brian rather somberly, until he said, "That all changed six months ago. I was visiting with a friend and told him how miserable I was in my marriage. He listened to my story and then gave me a copy of *The Five Love Languages.* He said, 'Read this. I think it will help you.'

"I went home and read it, cover to cover. As I read, it was like lightbulbs kept coming on in my brain. When I finished the book, I said to myself, 'Why didn't someone tell me this twenty years ago?' I realized that neither of us had been speaking the other's primary love language for at least twenty years. I gave the book to my wife and asked her to read it and let me know what she thought. The next week, we sat down and I said to her, 'Did that book make any sense to you?' She responded, 'I wish I had read it thirty years ago. I think it explains what went wrong in our marriage.' So I said to her, 'Do you think it would make any difference if we tried now?' to which she responded, 'We don't have anything to lose.' 'Does that mean you are willing to try?' I asked. 'Sure, I'll try,' she said.

"We discussed what we believed to be our primary love languages and agreed that with the help of God, we would seek to speak each other's primary love language at least once a week, no matter how we felt about each other. If anyone had told me that in two months I would have strong love feelings for my wife, I would have said, 'No way.' But I do."

At that point, Joanne broke into the conversation and said, "If anyone had told me that I would *ever* have love feelings for Brian again, I would have said it was impossible. But I do. It's like we are on a second honeymoon. Last month, we took the first vacation we have taken together in twenty years. It was wonderful. We enjoy being with each other again. My only regret is that we wasted twenty years. I realize now that both of us had such deep needs for love, and yet neither one knew how to meet the other's needs. I wish every couple could discover what we have discovered. It makes all the difference in the world."

Brian and Joanne speak for thousands of couples who have discovered that speaking their spouse's primary love language created a radically different atmosphere between the two of them. When they genuinely felt loved by their spouse, they were much more open to suggestions and requests.

It will be obvious that filling your spouse's love tank will take time, but not as much time as you might imagine. For Brian and Joanne, after living with empty love tanks for twenty years, the emotional climate changed within two months. You will not be ready to start requesting change until your spouse has lived with a full love tank for a few weeks. I cannot tell you how long it will take, but I can tell you how to know when you've arrived and are ready for the next step.

Several years ago, I devised a little game that has helped thousands of couples. It is called Tank Check. Here's the way you play the game: After you have been speaking your spouse's primary love language consistently for one month, ask your spouse, "On a scale of 0 to 10, how's the level in your love tank?" Wait for your spouse to give you a reading. If he or she says anything less than 10, you say, "What can I do to help fill it?" When your spouse gives you a suggestion, do it to the best of your ability. Play this game once a week. When you start getting responses of 8, 9, or 10 consistently, you will know you are ready for the next step, which is explained in the next chapter. I want you to read chapter 3 now so you can see where you're headed, but please don't try to implement the next step until you have completed the challenges of chapters 1 and 2.

TAKING ACTION

1. In your marriage, what do you complain about most often?

2. What does your spouse complain about most often?

3. With these answers in mind, guess which of the following love languages are most desired by your spouse. (Rank the following in order of importance, with the most desirable being number 1 and the least desirable being number 5.)

___ Words of Affirmation

___ Gifts

___ Acts of Service

___ Quality Time

___ Physical Touch

4. Now, using the same scale, indicate which love languages you would most like to receive:

___ Words of Affirmation

___ Gifts

___ Acts of Service

___ Quality Time

___ Physical Touch

5. If your spouse is willing, ask him or her to complete steps 1–4 above. Discuss your answers in order to discover each other's primary and secondary love languages. Choose to speak each other's primary and secondary love languages for the next month and see what happens.

6. If your spouse is not interested in participating in this Taking Action exercise, don't be discouraged. Instead, simply start speaking his or her primary and secondary love languages, based on your "best guesses" in number 3, above, and see what happens over the next month. Remember, love stimulates love.

3

Requesting Change

*H*ow can I get my spouse to change, without manipulation?" When you picked up this book, I assume this is what you really wanted to know. Perhaps you thought, *I'd even be willing to manipulate if I thought I could really get my spouse to change.* I understand the thought, but I really don't think that's what you want to do. Change that comes from manipulation is always accompanied by resentment. Resentment pushes people apart, and that is not what most couples want in their marriage.

Manipulation reduces a marriage relationship to the level of a contract negotiation: "If you'll do this, then I'll do that." At its worst, manipulation is simply an attempt by one spouse to control the other: "You will do this, or else." Perhaps the "or else" will induce enough fear in the spouse that he or she will acquiesce, but the change will be external and temporary. Real change comes from within, not from manipulating circumstances.

So how can you get real change? If you have read and applied what we've discussed in the first two chapters, you are now ready to request change from your spouse. The method of requesting change that I am about to describe will be effective only when you have genuinely dealt with your own past failures and you are expressing love in your spouse's primary love language. However, once you have established the proper foundation in your marriage relationship, real change is possible.

First, make a list of a few things you would sincerely like to see your spouse change.[†] It's important to be specific; generalities won't work. For example, "I want you to talk more" is too general and much

---

[†] At the end of the book, I have included sample lists of how husbands and wives have responded when asked the question, "What would you like to see your spouse change?"

too difficult to measure. If increasing your communication is the desired goal, say, "I want to request that we spend twenty minutes each evening—Monday through Friday—talking and listening to each other as we share our thoughts and feelings related to the events of the day." This request is specific, understandable, achievable, and measurable.

"I wish you would stop nagging me" is also far too nebulous. Pick one area in which you feel your spouse is nagging you and make a specific request related to that area. For example, you might say, "As you know, I have accepted the responsibility to take out the garbage. I would like to request that, in the future, you will not remind me of that task. I may not take it out on your timetable, but I will get rid of the garbage. When you keep reminding me, I feel like you are my mother and I am a child. I don't like that feeling, and I don't think it is good for our marriage. Therefore, I am requesting that you refrain from mentioning the garbage."

If you are the wife who hears this request, perhaps you would like to say to me, "Yes, but he won't take the garbage out. If I don't remind him, it will sit there for a week." My response to that is, "If you want to be married to a child, then continue to nag him about the garbage; but if you want to be married to an adult, then treat him like an adult. He will never act like an adult as long as you remind him of his responsibilities. And please, don't take the garbage out for him; that is an even greater insult. Spray the garbage with air freshener, but don't touch it. You will be amazed at what will happen."

All right, now that you have your specific requests in mind, are you ready to learn how to make requests of your spouse? Here are three suggestions for doing it right: Choose your setting, don't give an overdose of criticism, and precede your request with compliments.

CHOOSE YOUR SETTING

When you get ready to request a change from your spouse, it is extremely important that you choose your time and place and be sensitive to your spouse's emotional state. The time should be after a meal, never before a meal. When we are hungry, we are irritable—and when we are irritable, it is difficult to take suggestions. Have you noticed that when the family is on a trip together and everyone is hungry, everyone tends to be more argumentative? That the children are at each other's throats, and you find yourself yelling a lot more? That's because hunger and irritability are companions. When you are about to do something as important as requesting change from your spouse, be certain that it is not when he or she is hungry.

The place to make your request should always be in private, never in public. When you mention something you wish your spouse would change, and you do it in front of other people, it is a put-down, even if you couch it with humor. "My wife is not exactly a gourmet cook. Her specialty is hard-cooked, soft-boiled eggs." Everyone in the group may laugh, but your wife gets the barb. I hope you don't expect a soft-boiled egg anytime soon. It is more likely she'll want to throw a raw egg in your face when you walk into the kitchen the next morning. Put-downs only stimulate resentment and revenge.

If you want your spouse to accept your request, make it in private. Here's how one husband made a successful request after dinner one night: "Honey, I really appreciate the fact that you boil my eggs three mornings a week. I really like boiled eggs. My request is that on Wednesdays you try to make them soft boiled. I looked in a cookbook and it suggested that cooking the eggs for three minutes from the time the water starts boiling will produce a soft-boiled egg. If it would be helpful, I would be willing to buy a timer. It would mean a lot to me if one morning a week I could have my eggs soft boiled." This husband got his soft-boiled eggs.

A third part of the setting is your spouse's emotional state. Is he or she emotionally ready to receive a suggestion tonight? Some nights, we're emotionally drained. If everything we've done all day long has gone wrong, and if everyone we've met has been harping on us about something, the last thing we want when we get home is for our husband or wife to ask us to change something about ourselves. Even the simplest request can cause us to explode. Why? Because the request is the straw that breaks the camel's back.

How do you find out if your spouse is emotionally ready to receive a suggestion? The best way I know of is simply to ask. Say, "Honey, would this be a good night to make a request of you?" Even if your spouse says no, I can almost guarantee that he or she will be back in less than an hour, saying, "About that request. What did you have in mind?" He or she will be dying to know! But you say, "No, honey. It's not necessary tonight. We can do it on another night when you are feeling ready. You just let me know when you are feeling like it." Your spouse is likely to respond, "Well, I'm ready now." If that happens, then go ahead, because you have helped your spouse to get ready emotionally to receive your request. Don't ever hit your spouse broadside with a request for change. Always find out if he or she is emotionally ready to receive a suggestion.

DON'T GIVE AN OVERDOSE OF CRITICISM

Couples who don't have a system for requesting change will typically hold things inside that bug them, until the pressure gets so strong that they erupt in destructive criticism. A husband says, "I don't know why you can't record the checks that you write. Trying to balance the checkbook when half the records are missing is the most frustrating thing in the world." After launching this opening salvo, he continues, "And another thing: Why can't you leave my desk alone? I'm tired of trying to find things that you have moved. And while I'm at it, you left the garage door open again this morning. Can you imagine how much heat that wastes? And on the days when I'm out of town, does it ever cross your mind to bring in the mail? The box was stuffed last night when I opened it." Such overdoses of criticism almost never result in positive change.

Hostility gives birth to hostility. An overdose of inflammatory, condemning words will likely bring some return fire from the other spouse. "You're not exactly perfect yourself, you know. I can never depend on you for anything. You promised to bring me a sweatshirt the next time you went to Nashville, but you forgot it again. And I'm sick and tired of doing all the work around here. You don't ever lift a hand to help me. It's like you think I'm your slave. And I don't know how you have the gall to talk to me about leaving the garage door open when you never close a drawer in the bedroom."

Nothing constructive came of this conversation. The husband verbally shot his wife four times, she shot him back three times, and both spouses went away wounded and defensive. You can be certain that no positive changes will occur. Overdosing on criticism destroys the motivation for change.

I remember a husband who came to me a number of years ago and said, "I didn't come in here to get counseling. I came to tell you that I'm leaving my wife. I wanted you to hear it from me. I know that when I'm gone, she's going to call you, because she respects you. We've been married eight years, and I can't remember a single day in eight years that she hasn't criticized me. She criticizes the way I comb my hair, the way I walk, the way I talk, the way I dress, the way I drive. She doesn't like anything about me. I have finally concluded that if I'm all that bad, she deserves something better."

Later that day, when the wife called and came to my office, I shared with her what her husband had told me. She burst into tears and said, "I was just trying to help him."

Trying to help him? She decimated him. None of us can emotionally handle overdoses of criticism. All of us want change from our spouses, but overdosing on criticism is not the way to get it.

I suggest that you never make more than one request for change per week. That's fifty-two changes per year, and that ought to be enough. Some people are too emotionally fragile to handle even one request per week. For them, it may need to be one every two or three weeks. As you begin to develop the art of making requests, you may want to alternate weeks with your spouse. One week, you might make a request, and the next week it would be your spouse's turn. In fact, on the off weeks, I suggest that you *invite* your spouse to share something that he or she would like to see you change. When you and your spouse are home in the evening, after you've had dinner, you can say, "This would be a good night for you to give me a request for change. Tell me one thing that would make me a better spouse." Because you're the one who is initiating the conversation, you've predetermined your emotional state, and all that remains is to choose the right time and place to ask your spouse for a suggestion on how you can improve.

Personally, I find I can respond to one request per week from my wife, if it is made after a meal, in private, and when I am feeling emotionally stable. I want to be a better spouse and I can work on one thing a week, but more than that becomes overwhelming. Give me an overdose and I'm not likely to work on changing anything.

Perhaps you grew up in a home where you received overdoses of criticism. Every day, your parents told you what was wrong with you and what you needed to change. They seldom gave you compliments, but they filled your ears with condemning statements. Now that you're an adult and married, you may be giving your spouse overdoses of criticism without even realizing what you're doing, because you're just so used to it from your upbringing. You may want to ask your spouse, "Do you feel that I give you overdoses of criticism?" If he or she says yes, then I suggest that you apologize. Say that you're sorry and that you didn't realize what you were doing. After you've cleared the air, agree with your spouse that you will limit yourself to asking only once a week (or once every two weeks) for something you would like to see changed. And, of course, your spouse will have opportunities to make requests, as well.

Some couples have found the following technique helpful: If one partner starts to make a second request in the same week, the other person simply holds up two fingers and says, "Two, babe, two." Both agree that, when reminded, they will hold their second request until the next week. If you have a lot of things that are bugging you, you may want to get a little "request for change" notebook where you can write them all down. Each week, you can pick out one request to share with your spouse. Learning to limit the number of your requests makes the possibility of change more likely. When we are overwhelmed with requests, we tend to become resentful or angry, and these emotions do not foster change. Breaking the cycle of overdosing on criticism could save your marriage.

PRECEDE YOUR REQUEST
WITH COMPLIMENTS

Mary Poppins had it right when she sang, "A spoonful of sugar helps the medicine go down."[1] Compliments make the requests for change more palatable. I suggest a three-to-one ratio. Tell me three things you like about me, and then tell me one thing that you would like me to change.

Let's say that this week my wife is going to request of me that, before I leave the bathroom, I get the hairs out of the sink. Hairs in the sink bug her, and this is her week to make a request. But before she makes her request, she says to me, "Wait a minute, honey. First of all, I want you to know how much I appreciate the fact that you hang up your clothes. I have talked to other wives who tell me that their husbands leave clothes all over the house. Their wives have to pick up after them like they were children. You have always hung up your clothes. I guess your mother trained you—I don't know. But I like it.

"Second, I want you to know how much I appreciate the fact that last night you got the bugs off my windshield. I love it when you get the bugs off my windshield.

"And third, I want you to know how much I appreciate the fact that on Thursday nights you vacuum the floors. When you vacuum the floors, it is next door to heaven for me. One . . . two . . . three . . . are you ready, babe? Those hairs in the sink just bug me to death."

Now, I can work on cleaning up the hairs in the sink, and I probably will. Why? Karolyn likes me! Look, I'm already better than some guys (who can't pick up their clothes), and I want to be a better husband. I've seldom met a man who didn't want to be a better husband. I did meet one a while back. He said, "My wife doesn't deserve anything better." Perhaps, but most men would like to be better.

I'm suggesting that if a husband will take one request from his wife each week and will work on it to the best of his ability, he'll be amazed by how much better of a husband he'll become in three months. The same is true with wives who are willing to take a request from their husbands each week and seek to improve. In fact, I'll make a little prediction. If you will try this plan for requesting change, you'll walk in the door one day, maybe four months from now, and when you say to your spouse, "I'm ready for my suggestion of the week," your spouse will reply, "I think I'll pass this week."

Wow! Won't that be progress! From that point on, your spouse may not have a request every week. In fact, several weeks may pass between requests. But you'll always give your spouse a chance to make a request of you, to tell you something that would make you a better spouse.

Here's an important point: When you make a request and your spouse goes to work on it, don't forget to *notice* and *praise* the effort. Without compliments, your requests may sound like nagging. As one husband said, "I worked so hard at improving, and what did she do? Gave me another criticism! Once in a while, I'd like to know that I'm doing something right." By recognizing your spouse's efforts to improve and praising his or her positive qualities, you will motivate your spouse to make additional changes.

THINK ABOUT IT

When we get married, we discover all those things about the other person that we didn't know before. Some of those things really irritate us. They are flies in the ointment of our marital unity.

Perhaps you found out that when your husband takes a shower he leaves the washcloth in the bottom of the shower stall, sopping wet. When you walk by, you ask yourself, *Who does he think is going to pick that thing up?* Or maybe you discovered that your wife's clothes don't know how to get on hangers and her shoes don't know how to get to the closet.

You discover that he cannot brush his teeth without getting white spots on the mirror. When she replaces the bathroom tissue, she always puts it on backward. He always leaves the seat up. She squeezes the toothpaste in the middle, instead of on the bottom like she ought to. One husband told me, "I put a sign on our toothpaste: 'Squeeze my tail.' Didn't work!" he said.

What are you going to do about these irritations and the hundreds more that crop up over the years? I'm suggesting that once a week you request a change. And if it's something you're doing or not doing, and you can make a change, why not? Guys, if she wants the towels folded under and over, how long does it take to fold a towel under and over? Two seconds. A small price to pay for a happy wife. So your mother didn't fold towels under and over. You're not married to your mother. I believe we should change everything we can change to please each other. As we change, we make life easier for each other and we walk together in marital harmony.

WHAT ABOUT THE THINGS YOUR SPOUSE DOES NOT CHANGE?

It would be unfair of me to leave you with the impression that, if you follow the plan in this book, nine months or a year from now your spouse will do everything you request. In reality, there are some things your spouse cannot or will not change.

I can best illustrate this from my own life: Karolyn and I had been married for some time when I realized that she knew how to open drawers but didn't know how to close them. She also knew how to open cabinet doors but didn't know how to close them. And all these open drawers and doors bugged me.

One day, before I learned the things I have shared with you in this book, I said to her, "Karolyn, if you don't mind, when you finish in the kitchen could you please close the cabinet doors? I hit my head on these things if I'm not careful. And in the bathroom, when you finish, if you don't mind, would you please close the drawers? I catch my pants on these things when I walk through the room." To me, these were simple requests. The next day when I came home, I walked into our little apartment and glanced into the kitchen—and cabinet doors were open. I went into the bathroom, and drawers were open.

"OK, it's a habit," I reasoned. "It will take her awhile to change a habit so I will give her a few days."

I did. I gave her a week. But every day that week, I did my door check and my drawer check, and every day they were open.

At the end of the week, I thought to myself, *Maybe she didn't even hear what I said. Maybe she was having a bad day and really didn't get the message.* I was in graduate school in education, so I figured I'd just use a little education.

When I got home, I went into the bathroom, took everything out of the top drawer, and called Karolyn in for a demonstration. I opened the drawer and showed her how it worked. "This little wheel fits in this groove here. Marvelous things, these drawers. You could actually close this drawer with one finger." I demonstrated. Then I took Karolyn to the kitchen and said, "Now, if you get this door close enough, this little magnet here will grab it and close it for you."

I knew she got the message that day. When you use visual aids, you communicate, right? (I can hear all the wives booing me right now—and rightly so. But remember, I was young and foolish.)

The day after my little demonstration, when I came home from work, I walked into our apartment and glanced into the kitchen—and cabinet doors were open. I went into the bathroom, and drawers were open. Again I thought, *OK, it's a habit. It will take her awhile to change a habit. I'll give her a few days.* So I did; I gave her a month. But every day that month, I ran my door check and my drawer check, and every day they were open. At the end of a month, I gave Karolyn an angry lecture. I said, "I don't understand you. You're a college graduate. You are an intelligent woman. You are a deeply spiritual person, and yet you can't close drawers. I don't get it."

The problem persisted for nine months. I followed two approaches. For about a month or so, I would go on a "slow burn," which means I wouldn't say anything to Karolyn, but inside I was asking myself, *What is wrong with this woman?* Then I would switch and I would give her angry lectures for about a month. But it really didn't matter whether I gave her lectures or held it all inside; she did not close the drawers or the doors.

After nine months of this, I came home one night to find that our daughter, who was eighteen months old at the time, had stitches near the corner of one of her eyes.

"What happened?" I asked Karolyn. Amazingly, she told me the truth.

"She fell and cut herself on the corner of an open drawer."

I could not believe my ears. I thought to myself, *If I were you, I would not tell me that the baby fell onto an open drawer. Tell me anything else, but don't tell me she fell on an open drawer.* But Karolyn told me the truth.

I was so proud of myself for not overreacting. *I will not pour salt in the wound,* I said to myself. *I will not say, "I told you so."* But in my heart I was thinking, *I bet she'll close the drawers now!* And the other thought I had was, *She wouldn't listen to me. Now God is working on her.* But you know what? She still didn't close the drawers, even after that!

Two months later (this is now eleven months down the road), it finally dawned on me: *This woman will never close drawers.* I'm a slow learner, but I finally got the message. As my mind absorbed the full impact of this latest revelation, I went to the college library, sat down at my graduate study desk, and did what I had been trained to do. Have you heard this plan? When you don't know what to do about a problem, get a sheet of paper and write down all the thoughts that come to your mind—good thoughts, wild thoughts, crazy thoughts, helpful thoughts. Write them all down. Then go back and pick out your best alternative. That's what I did.

The first thing that came to my mind was this: *I could leave her.* I had thought about that before. On the heels of that idea came this thought: *If I ever get married again, the first thing I'm going to ask is, "Do you close drawers?"*

The second idea came in stages. I thought it through very carefully before I wrote it down: *I could be miserable—every time I see an open drawer—from now until the day I die, or she dies.* I thought it, so I wrote it.

The third possibility, and the last one I could think of, was this: *I could accept this as something she will never change, and from now on I could close the drawers myself.*

Since that time, some people who have heard the story have made other suggestions. One man told me that you can get springs that close the drawers automatically. (I didn't know that.) Another man told me that he had taken the cabinet doors off altogether. (That thought never crossed my mind.)

When I was done, I looked at my list and marked off number 1 immediately. I was in seminary, studying to be a pastor. I thought, *If I leave her, I'll never get a pastorate.* So I marked that one off quickly. I read number 2 and also marked it off. I thought, *Why would a grown man choose to be miserable about something for the rest of his life?* That didn't make sense.

Well, that left me with number 3. I could accept the fact that my wife would never change, and from this point on I could close the drawers myself. Then I asked myself, "How long would it take me to close the cabinet doors in the kitchen?"

One . . . two . . . three . . . four seconds.

"How long would it take me to close the drawers in the bathroom?"

One . . . two . . . three seconds.

"Four plus three equals seven. *Seven seconds.* I believe I can work that into my schedule."

When I got home, I said to Karolyn, "About those drawers . . ."

She quickly responded, "Gary, please don't bring that up again!"

"No," I said, "babe, no, no, I've got an answer. From now on, and for as long as I'm alive, you will never have to close the doors or the drawers again. From now on, I'll close the doors, I'll close the drawers, and you won't ever have to worry about it."

Do you know what she said?

"Fine."

And she walked out of the room. It was no big deal to her, but it was a major turning point in my life. Ever since that day, open drawers have not bothered me. I have no emotion when I see an open drawer. In fact, if you were to walk with me into our bathroom most nights, you'd see that the drawers are open. But when I walk in, I close them—because that's my job!

What am I saying? I'm saying there will be a few things that your spouse either cannot or will not change. I don't know which it is, and it really doesn't matter. I have an incredibly wonderful wife. She has made many changes for me. I have often thought that maybe it's something genetic that prevents her from closing drawers. It's possible! But whether it's *can't* or *won't*, the point is that your spouse will never fulfill all your requests.

So, what are you going to do about the things your spouse won't change? I believe that love accepts these imperfections.[2] Wouldn't I be foolish, after all these years, to still be mumbling and grumbling about open drawers? Instead, I choose to thank God for all the positive changes that Karolyn has made, and I choose to accept the things that she either cannot or will not change.

Some of you men have been running behind your wives for fifteen years mumbling about the lights. "I don't understand why you can't turn off the lights when you leave a room. The switch works both ways, you know. And it just takes one finger. If you would turn off the lights, I could buy you a new coat." I don't want to discourage you, guys, but if she hasn't turned off the lights for fifteen years, she may never. Maybe you need to understand that she is the "light turner-onner" and you are the "light turner-offer." Love accepts some imperfections. (And aren't you glad?)

By now you realize that I'm not promising you that your spouse will change everything to your satisfaction. What I am saying is that if you will implement the three-step plan I've outlined in this book, your spouse will make significant changes. I have never seen the plan fail. Here is a recap:

Step One: *Confess your own failures and ask forgiveness.* This sends a clear signal that you realize you have not been a perfect spouse in the past. It indicates that you are thinking seriously about your marriage and that you want the relationship to improve. Whether or not your spouse is able to forgive you immediately, he or she is now aware that something significant is happening in your mind. This awareness plants a seed of hope.

Step Two: *Learn to speak your spouse's primary love language.* When confession is followed by new expressions of unconditional love in your spouse's primary love language, you are watering that seed of hope. You are meeting your spouse's emotional need for love in the most effective way. In due time, the sprout of new life will emerge. Those expressions of love will stimulate emotional warmth and change the climate in your marriage. You may begin to see a new sparkle in your spouse's eyes, and a more positive attitude toward you and your marriage. Eventually your spouse will begin to reciprocate by expressing love to you in your primary love language. That's when you'll discover that nothing holds more potential in human relationships than the power of unconditional love.

Step Three: *Now you are ready to begin making specific requests.* Because your spouse has already forgiven you for your past failures, and because your spouse already feels your love, he or she will be far more open to your requests. Most people are willing to make changes when they feel loved.

What has been interesting to me through the years is that couples who implement this plan often find their spouse making positive changes even before they are requested. Because of past complaints, they already know many of the changes that their husband or wife desire. Now that they are living in an atmosphere of forgiveness and are experiencing their spouse's expressions of love, they are motivated to do things that they think their spouse will appreciate—without even being asked.

"I couldn't believe it," one husband said. "For years, I had asked my wife to walk the dog one night a week while I attended the Elk's Club. She never did it. I always hated coming home on Tuesday nights at 9:30 and having to walk the dog. I was about six weeks into the 'love phase' of this new strategy when I came home one Tuesday night and discovered that she had already walked the dog. I hadn't even gotten around to requesting it. I was blown away. I told her how much I appreciated it.

From that night on, she has always walked the dog on Tuesday nights. I know it's a little thing, but it means a lot to me."

Little changes or big changes, they are all easier when past failures have been confessed and love has become a way of life. Now that you have read this little book and have a clear picture of how to get your spouse to change without manipulation, I want to challenge you to implement the program. Read chapter 1 again, and begin the process of identifying and confessing your past failures. Don't rush the process. Take time to get outside help, as described in the chapter. Make your confession thorough and genuine. Then reread chapter 2, discover your spouse's primary love language, and begin speaking it regularly. Two weeks into the process, start to sprinkle in the other four love languages as well. Then play the Tank Check game with your spouse. When you are receiving consistent scores of 8, 9, or 10, you will know that you are ready to begin making your requests for change.

When you start to see positive changes in your spouse, I would love to hear your story. Visit www.garychapman.org and select the Contact link. I hope to hear from you soon.

⌒

TAKING ACTION

1. Think of times in the past when you or your spouse gave each other overdoses of criticism. How did you feel? How do you think your spouse felt?

2. Think of times in the past when your spouse verbalized something that he or she wanted changed, but did it in the presence of other people. How did it make you feel? Or, if you were the one who verbalized something about your spouse, how do you think it made him or her feel?

3. In the future, if your spouse agreed to make his or her request in private, after a meal, and after giving you three compliments, how often would you be willing to receive a request?

    ____ one request for change per week

____ one request for change every two weeks

____ other (please specify):

_____

4. If your spouse is willing, ask him or her to complete steps 1–3 above. Discuss your answers and begin following the plan for requesting change suggested in this chapter.

5. If your spouse is not interested in participating in this Taking Action exercise, don't be discouraged. Simply tell him or her that you would like to work on becoming a better mate and would like for him or her to give you one suggestion each week (or every other week) for something you could change that would make your spouse's life easier. (When your spouse sees that you are taking the requests for change seriously, he or she is likely to begin reciprocating.)

6. Make a list of a few things you would sincerely like to see your spouse change. (At the end of the book, I have included

sample lists of how husbands and wives have responded when asked the question, "What would you like to see your spouse change?")

7. Now, go over this list and make sure your requests are specific, understandable, and achievable. The more specific, the better. (You may want to read pages 58–59 again.)

8. Remember:

   - Never make more than one request per week (or according to your agreed-upon schedule).

   - Never make a request when your spouse is hungry.

   - Always make your request in private.

   - Ask if your spouse is emotionally ready for you to make your request.

   - Precede your request with at least three compliments.

*I*n my own life and in the lives of hundreds of couples I have counseled, the principles in this book have brought real change. It is my hope that you will now do the hard work of implementing this three-fold approach. You have the plan. It has worked for other couples, and I'm encouraging you to try it in your own marriage. You have nothing to lose and everything to gain. And if it works for you, I hope you will share it with your friends. In today's cultural climate, successful marriages are more difficult than ever to effect. I believe the ideas shared in this book have the potential for helping thousands of couples move down the road of marital intimacy with greater harmony. If that happens, I will be greatly pleased.

SOME THOUGHTS WORTH REMEMBERING

- The most common reason people do not get the changes they desire is that they start at the wrong place.

- Most of us have lived by the philosophy, "If my spouse would change, then I would change." If most of us are honest, we will have to admit this approach has not worked.

- Confessing wrong liberates us from the bondage of past failures and opens up the possibility for changed behavior in the future.

- Confession of wrongdoing needs to be broader than simply confessing to God. You also need to confess to the person you have wronged. In marriage, that is your spouse.

- We cannot erase past failures, but we can agree that what we did or failed to do was wrong, and we can sincerely ask for forgiveness. In so doing, we are starting at the right place.

- One of the fundamental languages of love is to speak words that affirm the other person. Affirming words give life, while condemning words bring death.

- A gift is a physical, visible token of thoughtfulness. Any adult can learn to give gifts.

- For some people, "Actions speak louder than words." Doing something that you know your spouse would like for you to do is an expression of love.

- Quality time is much more than being in the same room or the same house with your spouse. It involves giving your spouse your undivided attention.

- All requests for change should be specific, understandable, doable, and measurable.

- Tell me three things you like about me, and then tell me one thing you would like for me to change. Compliments make the request more palatable.

- I believe we should change everything we can change to please each other. As we change we make life easier for each other and we walk together in marital harmony.

HOW TO GET YOUR SPOUSE TO CHANGE WITHOUT MANIPULATION

A Three-Step Plan

Step 1. Start by admitting your own past failures and request forgiveness.

Step 2. Discover your spouse's primary love language and speak it daily

Step 3. When making a request for change,

    a. Choose your setting (time, place, emotional climate):

       Time—after a meal;

       Place—in private; or

       Emotional climate—when your spouse gives you permission.

b. Don't give an overdose of criticism (never more than one request per week, or according to the schedule to which you and your spouse have agreed).

c. Give three compliments before you make your request.

d. When your spouse works to make a change, *notice* and *express appreciation.* Accept those things that your spouse cannot or will not change.

This is a collection of what husbands have said when asked the question, "What would you like to see your wife change?" Some of these are specific and others are too general to be helpful. They are presented here simply to stimulate your thinking as you make a list of the things you would like to request of your wife. (Remember: Limit your requests to one per week, or according to your agreement with your wife.)

I wish she would not snap at our children.

I wish she would share more of her dreams and fears with me.

I wish she would spend thirty minutes a day
talking with me.

I wish she would keep the kitchen desk
organized.

I wish she would not clean and fuss with the
house when I'm home.

I wish she would develop more confidence in her
appearance and be willing to wear "sexy"
clothing.

I wish she would stop bringing up the past.

I wish she would stop trying to control my
thoughts and activities by making demands.

I wish she would not worry so much.

I wish she would stop being my mother
(e.g., reminding me to brush my teeth).

I wish she would look for positive things rather
than focusing on the negative.

I wish she would answer my questions with an
answer rather than another question.

I wish she would tell me that she admires me.

I wish she would tell me that she is attracted to me.

I wish she would wash and clean the truck every week.

I wish she would talk to me.

I wish she would clean up after herself.

I wish she would stop criticizing me in front of our children.

I wish she would start getting ready earlier so we could arrive at our destination on time.

I wish she would relax and enjoy life more (e.g., watch TV with me).

I wish she would initiate sexual intercourse when she is in the mood, because I'm almost always in the mood.

I wish she would put her clothes away instead of leaving them on the floor.

I wish she would stop being so critical.

I wish she would keep the car cleaner.

I wish she would start working out at the gym and get in shape.

I wish she would learn to go to sleep with the light on so I can read.

I wish she would become more aware of the health problems related to her weight.

I wish she would get rid of some junk.

I wish she would tend to the housekeeping on a more routine basis.

I wish she would help me teach our children the value of work.

I wish she would let me cook more often.

I wish she would quit being angry all the time and have more patience with me and other people.

I wish she had a higher sex drive.

I wish she would keep the animals under better control.

I wish she would stick to her goals, even though it may be uncomfortable.

I wish she would speak kindly to me and about others.

I wish she would allow me to express my opinion even if she disagrees with me.

I wish she would not question my decisions in areas that are not her expertise, such as buying new tires for the car.

I wish she would be more intimate in bed.

I wish she would praise my hard work and say other nice things every day.

I wish she would stop putting me down.

I wish she would not be so critical and condescending toward me and start giving me more affirmation.

I wish she would not drive herself so hard— work hours, business, church.

I wish she would stop interrupting me when
we have a discussion.

I wish she would give me a big kiss each morning
before I leave the house.

I wish she would learn to discuss difficult issues
without becoming defensive and interpreting
everything as personal criticism.

I wish she would give me a back rub three times
a week.

I wish she would drink Starbucks.

I wish she would stay awake when I'm talking
with her.

I wish she were more comfortable leaving our
children with babysitters so we could do some
fun things together.

This is a collection of what wives have said when asked the question, "What would you like to see your husband change?" Some of these are specific and others are too general to be helpful. They are presented here simply to stimulate your thinking as you make a list of the things you would like to request of your husband. (Remember: Limit your requests to one per week, or according to your agreement with your husband.)

I wish he would sit down each evening and talk with me for ten minutes.

I wish he would clean the garage and keep it clean.

I wish he would take nightly walks with me.

I wish he would watch ESPN less.

I wish he would not go from 0 to 60 miles per hour in 2.4 seconds when he is angry.

I wish he would help me give the girls a bath.

I wish he would help me pick up and keep the house cleaner.

I wish he were able to accept some feedback from me. He is extremely sensitive to any comments that may be less than 100 percent positive.

I wish he would not fall asleep when I talk.

I wish he would stop smoking.

I wish he would plan date nights once or twice a month.

I wish he would give me his undivided attention

(put down the paper, crossword puzzle, etc.) when I am trying to talk with him.

I wish he would not procrastinate. "I'll do it tomorrow" is his theme.

I wish he would express appreciation for me and what I do.

I wish he would play more with the children.

I wish he would stop piling papers on the table or clear it off regularly.

I wish he would be less critical of my housework.

I wish he would stop dropping stuff all over the house, starting when he walks in the front door, and leaving stuff where it is dropped.

I wish he would spend more time considering what is important to me.

I wish he would be more frugal with our money and work with me on developing a plan to repay our debts.

I wish he would start picking up the clutter in

the house instead of telling me that we need to pick up the clutter in the house.

I wish he would have a ten-minute devotional time with me each day, reading the Bible and praying.

I wish he would ask me what he could do to help me out around the house.

I wish he would let me express my feelings without reacting in anger.

I wish he would speak more kindly to me.

I wish he would turn off the TV and talk with me for a few minutes.

I wish he would exercise with me and try to get in shape.

I wish he would take more pains in washing the windshield and windows in the car.

I wish he would stop "tooting" at the table.

I wish he would pick up his shoes in the bedroom and put them in the closet.

I wish he would talk with me about decisions
  before he makes them. I'd like to be a partner
  and work as a team.

I wish he would come to bed the same time I do
  so that we could talk and sometimes make
  love together.

I wish he would make an effort to speak proper
  English. He frequently uses wrong tenses,
  which makes him appear stupid. He is very
  intelligent.

I wish he would learn decent eating etiquette.

I wish he would give me some time to be alone.
  He is wonderful and helpful. I just need some
  time to be by myself.

I wish he would compliment what I do and how
  I look, and encourage me.

I wish he would put things away when he finishes
  a project.

I wish he would stop rescuing our daughters

(ages 18 and 20). Let them experience the consequences of their choices.

I wish he would devote as much time, energy, love, and devotion to me as he does to his work and exercise program. I feel like I get what is left at the end of a busy day—and that's not much.

I wish he would put his arms around me and hold my hand when we walk.

I wish he would initiate more dates with me.

I wish he would mow the grass before the yard becomes unsightly.

I wish he would stop swearing when he gets angry.

I wish he would spend quality time with God, me, and our children.

I wish he would hug me and touch me, even when it doesn't lead to sex.

I wish he would take the responsibility for handling our personal finances.

I wish he would find some good friends or

activities that would allow him some recreational time away from me occasionally. That would allow me to have some girlfriend time without feeling guilty.

I wish he would earn enough money so that I didn't have to work full time.

I wish he would look intently into my eyes and talk for longer than five minutes.

I wish he would defend me or stand up for me with his parents.

⌒ *Notes*

CHAPTER 1

1. Author's paraphrase of Matthew 7:3-5.

2. Psalm 139:23-24, NLT.

3. 1 John 1:9.

4. For more information on the topic of rebuilding trust, see Gary D. Chapman, *The Five Languages of Apology* (Chicago: Northfield Publishing, 2006).

CHAPTER 2

1. Ollie Jones, "Love Makes the World Go Round," 1958.

2. Gary D. Chapman, *The Five Love Languages* (Chicago: Northfield Publishing, 1992, 1995, 2004).

CHAPTER 3

1. Richard M. Sherman and Robert B. Sherman, "A Spoonful of Sugar," from the movie *Mary Poppins*.

2. 1 Peter 4:8.

About the Author

Dr. Gary Chapman is the author of the perennial best seller *The Five Love Languages* (more than 3.5 million copies sold) and numerous other marriage and family books. He is currently working with best-selling author Catherine Palmer on a new fiction series based on *The Four Seasons of Marriage*, the first book of which is scheduled to release in the spring of 2007. Dr. Chapman is the director of Marriage and Family Life Consultants, Inc.; an internationally known speaker; and the host of *A Growing Marriage*, a syndicated radio program heard on more than 100 stations across North America. He and his wife, Karolyn, live in North Carolina.

DO YOU KNOW WHICH SEASON
YOUR MARRIAGE IS IN?

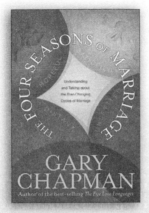

Every marriage goes through different seasons—
the satisfaction and security of summer, the
hopefulness and anticipation of spring, the
change and uncertainty of fall, and the icy
bitterness of winter. Find out which season your
marriage is currently in and learn the strategies
that will strengthen your relationship through
every season of marriage.

❧

Available now in stores and online!

Take the free marriage-satisfaction quiz at
www.4seasonsofmarriage.com

CONFLICT IS INEVITABLE.
ARGUING IS A CHOICE.

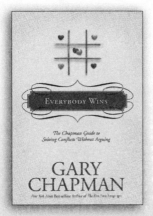

Relationship expert Dr. Gary Chapman provides a
simple blueprint to help you and your spouse find
win-win solutions to the everyday disagreements that
crop up in every marriage. Solving conflict without
arguing will leave you and your spouse feeling loved,
listened to, and appreciated.